BLACK CAT BONE

BLACK CAT BONE

John Burnside

CAPE POETRY

Published by Jonathan Cape 2011

6 8 10 9 7

First published in Great Britain in 2011 by
Jonathan Cape
Random House, 20 Vauxhall Bridge Road,
London SW1V 2SA

www.rbooks.co.uk

Addresses for companies within The Random House Group Limited can be found at:
www.randomhouse.co.uk/offices.htm

The Random House Group Limited Reg. No. 954009

A CIP catalogue record for this book
is available from the British Library

ISBN 9780224093859

The Random House Group Limited supports The Forest Stewardship Council (FSC®),
the leading international forest certification organisation. Our books carrying the FSC
label are printed on FSC® certified paper. FSC is the only forest certification scheme
endorsed by the leading environmental organisations, including Greenpeace.
Our paper procurement policy can be found at www.randomhouse.co.uk/environment

Typeset in Bembo by Palimpsest Book Production Limited,
Falkirk, Stirlingshire
Printed and bound in Great Britain by
MPG Books Ltd, Bodmin, Cornwall

for David Miller

CONTENTS

THE FAIR CHASE

De torrente in via bibet;
propterea exaltabit caput
Psalm 109

What we were after there, in the horn and vellum
shadows of the wood behind our house,
I never knew.

At times, it felt like bliss, at times
a run of musk and terror, gone to ground
in broken wisps of ceresin and chrism,

but now and then, the beast was almost there,
glimpsed through the trees,
or lifting its head from a stream

to make us out:
a coarseness on the wind
and brittle voices sifted from the morning.

We tracked the scent through barley fields and hollows,
we followed it into the spinney
with billhooks and sickles,

but nothing was ever there, save the codling moon
and, far in the meadows,
the one field of nothing but grasses

where something had lain,
in a fetor of blood-warmth and pollen,
before it moved on.

Still, we continued;
when one man sickened and died,
another would take his place in the wandering column,

blacksmiths and lawyers, orchardmen,
butchers in waiting,
lost in the fog, or hallooing after the pack,

3

and all of them friends of my father's; though, needless to say,
in a country like this, the dead have more friends
than the living.

We were the men you saw
on a winter's morning:
cumbersome bodies, shrouded in gunsmoke and cyan,

we went out every day, in every season,
falconers, rat catchers, deerstalkers, whippers-in,
plucking at shadows, purblind, afraid of our dogs,

and if, on occasion, I never quite saw the point,
I was always the first to arrive, with my father's gun,
bound to the old ways, lost in a hand-me-down greatcoat

and last among equals – flycatcher, dreamer, dolt,
companion to no one,
alone in a havoc of signs.

*

One year, the reservoir froze.
I walked out to the centre of the ice
and gazed down through a maze of gills and weed

to where a god I'd read about in books
– sweeter than pine, but stone-hard in his tomb –
lay waiting for a gaze to curse with knowledge.

The ice was clear as glass: I hunkered in
and dared him, from that unreflecting world,
to pull me through, in one bright flash of rage,

no crack, no sudden drop into the cold,
nothing to witness,
nothing to remember.

Minutes I waited; then the others came
and called me back, the dogs a swarm of noise
and worry, old men's

faces in a mist of their own breath
ashamed for my father's sake
and his father before him.

We carried on; I walked off to one side,
and halfway through the white of afternoon,
I slipped away, unwanted, or unnoticed,

taking a road less-travelled through fields and yards
of stunted brassicas and rotting tyres,
strangers in coveralls or leather aprons

stopping to watch as I passed: no hand raised in greeting,
no dog come out
to see me on my way.

That was a foreign country: snowdrifts, then sand,
blotted and kissed with yew-drupes
and windfall holly,

spotted owls hunting for beetles along the hedge,
smoke in the distance, nether roads,
passing bells.

I walked for hours, yet it was light as noon
when I came to a place I thought I had seen before
through a lull in the weather:

nothing to speak of,
a dirt track and sheep in the woods,
and that sense of a burial, under the moss and ruin,

but something was present a few steps into the treeline,
one of those creatures you find in a children's album,
a phantom thing, betrayed by smoke or rain,

or glimpsed through a gap in the fog, not quite discerned,
not quite discernible: a mouth, then eyes,
then nothing.

It lingered a while;
and then, as if it wanted me to play,
it shifted away through the trees – and I followed after.

Crashing through cover, ducking through sumac and maple
it leapt and ran, though never so fast or so far
that I couldn't keep pace

and when I paused for breath, it also paused
and stayed,
as if it wanted me to follow.

I never saw it clear, but it was there:
sometimes the brown of a roe-deer, sometimes
silver, like a flight of ptarmigan,

it shifted and flickered away
in the year's last light
and I came after, with my heavy gun,

trudging for miles
through meadows laced with rime,
working by scent

and instinct, finally
true to myself,
with the body and mind of a hunter

and, by the time I stepped into a glade
candy-striped with light and frosted grass,
I knew exactly what a man should do

in my position – lucky, singled out
by death and beauty for the blessèd kill,
assenting to the creature's dumb assent

to blood and darkness
and the life
beyond.

I took a bullet,
loaded it with care
and aimed with an intent that felt like love,

though I only knew love
by hearsay
and stubborn lack.

No sound, no movement; all the world was still
and not a creature in it
but ourselves,

me taking aim
and the animal stopped in its tracks,
waiting to see what would happen, unafraid,

a deer, I thought, and then I saw a fox,
and thinking I knew what it was
I pulled the trigger.

★

The old days were better for mourning;
better for tongue-tacked women
in ruined plaid

climbing a hillside
to gather the rainwashed bones
of what they had lost, that winter, to the cold,

and men in the prime of their lives,
with dwindled sight,
dreaming all night of that slow white out by the river

where, once or twice a year,
a girl would drown,
pledging her heart to a boy she had mostly imagined.

I remembered the flow country, then,
as the gunsmoke darkened:
I'd go there as a child on Sabbath days,

my father asleep in his church clothes, a fret of chickens
wandering back and forth
at the kitchen door,

a lull in the house and that emptiness high in the roof
as if someone had frittered away
in a summer wind.

I'd go out in my Sunday clothes and shoes
to the shimmer and dart
of sticklebacks threading the light

and search for something I could never name,
the blue of a smile, or the curious
pleasure of the doomed, as they go under;

and that was what I hurried out to see,
crossing the space
to where the beast went down

but all I could find when I got there, standing dismayed
in the stopped air of afternoon, with smoke on my lips
and my heart like a fettered thrush in the well of my throat,

all I could find was an inkwash of blear in the grass
like the fogged stain after a thaw,
and a ribbon of musk

threading away to the trees
and the distance beyond:
no body, no warmth, no aftermath, nothing to prize,

and the night coming down all at once,
like a weight at my shoulders,
settling in waves, till all I could see was my hands.

★

Everyone becomes
the thing he kills
– or so the children whisper, when they crush

a beetle or a cranefly in the dust,
feeling the snuff of it bleed
through the grain of their fingers;

I'd always thought of that
as superstition:
a wishful thinking, how the spirit moves

from one shape to the next
like breath,
or warmth,

infinite kinship, laid down in the blood
against the sway
of accident and weather;

yet out in the woods that night, as I dug myself in
to wait for the day, I felt it in my gut,
a gravity I'd never known before

dragging me down
so it seemed I would cleave to the earth,
the life I had taken

snug as a second skin.
I should have died, if not for the faint warmth
that held me there, unseeing, in a night

so utter, dawn
was like a miracle:
the trees emerging, piecemeal, from the cold,

a snowflake here, then there, then everything
arriving all at once, as I awoke
and, never having slept, began to walk.

I didn't know how far I was from home,
but nothing looked familiar
– not the woods

and not the road I found that afternoon,
dizzy from cold and hunger, hurrying on
through empty yards and desolate plantation,

nothing alive
as far as the eye could see,
only the white of the sky, like a wondering gaze

pursuing me from one field to the next,
from ditch to ditch,
from wall to broken wall.

I walked like that for days. The road led on
through spruce and lodgepole pine, then dipped away
to where a village lay, warmed in a crook

of hills that seemed familiar, suddenly:
a spill of lights and woodsmoke and a kirk
that made me think of something in a book

before I made it out. My dead were there
among the tilted stones;
I knew the market cross; I knew the spire;

but everything was strange, even the house
I came to at the far end of the lane
that passed the abattoir then crossed the brook

and finished at the unclipped cypress hedge
where no one lived next door,
though there were ghosts,

so frail, I only knew them by the sound
the wind made
when it worried at the shutters.

★

Nobody lives
here now, it's only
crows and bees

and every shift
and slant
is an event,

historic
in its void
of mud and wire.

Yet now and again
I have turned
in a falling shadow

and caught a glimpse
of something
at my back,

not heard, or seen,
but felt,
the way some distant

shiver in the barley registers,
before I can think to say
it was never there.

The hunters pass at daybreak, casting
curious looks at my door, but no one is here
to see, as they enter the mist

and disappear.
Nobody lives here now, not even me,
and yet the house is mine – a net of dreams

and phantoms
and that living animal
I followed through the woods: locked in my bones

and calling for the life it must have had
far in the green of the pines, and the white of the snow,
where I am hunting, hunting even now,

hearing that cry
and turning my head,
for an echo.

EVERAFTER

Bitte betrachten Sie mich als einen Traum!

Franz Kafka (remark to Adolf Brod)

ON THE FAIRYTALE ENDING

Begin with the fend-for-yourself
of all the loves you learned about
in story books;

fish-scale and fox-print
graven on the hand
forever
        and a tiny hook-and-eye

unfastened in the sweetmeat of a heart
you thought would never grieve
or come undone.

May; and already
it's autumn: broken gold
and crimson in the medieval

beechwoods, where our shadows come and go,
no darker
than the figures in a book

of changes,
till they're hexed
and singled out

for something chill and slender in this world,
more sleight-of-hand
than sorrow or safekeeping.

DISAPPOINTMENT

*Hope will predominate in every mind, till it has been
suppressed by frequent disappointments.*

Samuel Johnson

I turn left out of the rain
at Kippo junction,
the windshield clearing to sky and a skim
of swallows over the road like the last few
pages of a 50s story book

where someone is walking home
to the everafter,
touched with the smell of the woods and the barberry
shadows where the boy he left behind
is standing up to his waist in a Quink-blue current,

a burr of water streaming through his hands
in silt italics, touch all hook-and-eye
beneath the swell, and fingers opened wide
to catch what slithers past – the powder-blue
and neon of a surer life than his,

scant as it is, and lost, in the gaze of others.

LOVED AND LOST

Give me a childhood again and I will live
as owls do, in the moss and curvature

of nightfall
                    – glimpsed,
but never really seen,

tracking the lane
to a house I have known from birth

through goldenrod
and alstrœmeria;

while somewhere,
at the far edge of the day,

a pintailed duck
is calling to itself

across a lake,
                    the answer it receives

no more or less remote than we become
to one another,

                    mapped,
then set aside, till we admit

that love divulged is barely love at all:
only the slow decay of a second skin

concocted from the tinnitus of longing.

'A GARDEN INCLOSED IS MY SISTER, MY SPOUSE'

Matthew 22:14

Give me the medieval
lull of the sexless, praying behind a smile,

the eyes forever
slicked in candlelight

and all the world
in waiting: fields

of ammonite and bronze beneath the sway
of pasture, chalk

and charnel in the far room of a mind

that never sleeps, and will not let itself
be gathered to its god, no swarm and *noir*,

no slow extinction
filtered through the clouds,

but one thing, then another: green, then black;
hair in the lark's tongue, marrow in the pine.

THE BRIDE

And Samson said unto her, If they bind me
with seven green withs that were never dried,
then shall I be weak, and be as another man.
                                   Judges 16: 7

Whatever you should have been, you were never the one
who walked home from the small hours in a veil
of citrus and mariposa, dressed for another
ballo in maschera,

though someone who looks like you is the woman I spin
from willow and *L'air du temps* for the qualified world
to paralyse with echoes from the Book
of Judges, bowls

of watermark and blood set out to fade
beneath a yellow moon, while you remove
first one ring, then the next, your vows unlocked
and scattered in the dark, *qual pium' al vento.*

THE NIGHTINGALE

I

Under der linden
an der heide,
dâ unser zweier bette was,
dâ muget ir vinden
schône beide
gebrochen bluomen unde gras.
Vor dem walde in einem tal,
tandaradei,
schône sanc diu nahtegal.
   Walther von der Vogelweide

If not the bridegroom or the Well-Beloved,
there's something here that chooses to remain

through centuries of thorn
and Lindenbaum,

to sing, not with the grace
of flesh surpassed,

but rain-deep, in the hollow of the stem,
where darkness folds and blisters into foreign

bodies, galls
and knots of keratin,

hunger and the thousand forms of lust
that quicken out of matter, fire-

and sap-stained, songs
unwinding from the throat

as breath spills out and comes, time and again,
to nothing – neither echo nor lament –

the buds we wreathed in silk, for wedding nights,
discarded now, a summer's lease of green

gone back beneath the frost while, nonetheless,
alone in the furthest wood, a night bird sings

and sings unheard,
where once we made our bed.

II

We lie where we made our bed, through years of rent
and kidskin, you

in indigo, the uncontested Queen
of soap-and-water, Low-Cal, mezzotint

epiphanies for Michaelmas
and Lent.

I come home late and vanish on the stairs;
you riffle through the Deaths and Marriages

for something more akin
to passion spent,

and when you leave me so,
unsatisfied,

I lumber on, by mutual consent,
whole flocks of shadow papering my skin

with scuffs and stains
and film clips of ascent.

NOTES TOWARDS AN ENDING

No more conversations.
                    No more wedlock.
No more vein of perfume in a scarf
I haven't worn for months, her voice come back
to haunt me, and the Hundertwasser sky
Magnificat to how a jilted heart
refuses what it once mistook for mercy.

It's never what we wanted, everafter;
we asked for something else, a lifelong Reich
of unexpected gifts and *dolce vita,*
peach-blossom smudging the glass and a seasoned
glimmer of the old days in this house
where, every night, we tried and failed to mend
that feathered thing we brought in from the yard,
after it came to grief on our picture window.

BLACK CAT BONE

E il naufragar m'è dolce in questo mare
Leopardi

NATIVITY

I come by chance. A train slows in the fog
and stands a while

and, when it leaves, there's one more soul aboard,
sung from the quiet, passing from car to car,
like the angel of God;

or, north of here, in some old lumber town,
the church clock stops, the wind dies in the trees

and I lie squalling in a slick of blood
and moonlight, seventh son
to some man's seventh son.

No gifts for me, no angel in the rafters
caught like a bird in the updraft from the stove,

only the words of an old curse scratched on the wall,
and the warmth of my mother
fading, as lights go out

in house after house, from here
to the edge of the world,

her slack mouth, then the darkness in her eyes
the first thing I see
when the midwife returns with a candle.

DEATH ROOM BLUES

Before the songs I sang there were the songs
they came from, patent shreds
of Babel, and the secret
Nineveh of back rooms in the dark.

Hour after hour
the night trains blundered through
from towns so far away and innocent
that everything I knew seemed fictional:

the squares of light beyond the paper mill
where wolves crept from the woods and found their way
to soft spots in the slick of memory;

the boy who killed his mother in her bed
for Jesus' sake.

Small wonder that I overcame my fear
of sweetness, when the only white I knew
was first snow at the margins of the world,

and any chore is sweeter, now,
than scripture, where the hand that smoothes away
each local asterisk of stripped desire

can seem so much like something I once lost
I'm half convinced that childhood never happened.

TRANSFIGURATION

I found a bobcat dying in the road
and stole the tattered remnant
of its soul.
I hunkered down and leaned into its last
sour breath, to drink it in:
I tasted blood and catpiss and a thread
of spirit in my throat, like gasoline.

I was the Alpha, driving in the rain
from town to town, unravelling the gospel.
I was the Omega, falling asleep at the wheel
and travelling on unharmed, through dreams of musk
and fur, no final wave
of son or husband buried in my hands,
my blood exchanged for fire, my thoughts for stone.

DOPE HEAD BLUES

I live in a separate country, white as the snow
on rooftops and stained glass

windows, the still of the woods
at furthest noon the only thought I have

and morphine skimming my mind, like the first
swallow in the courtyard, high and small

the voice, as if it came
from somewhere else;

and somewhere else, the house of rain and corn
that glimmers in the dark, while I ascend

to morning, warmth
and daylight, like the shirt a man

lies down in, after a long
unshrouding, seams

unstitching in my heart,
the taste of me the taste of something other.

HURTS ME TOO

I love my love with an X
                        and the black cat bone
she buries in a kiss is sweeter now
than honey from the book of Genesis.

Rain on the yards; a cuckoo in the meadows;
I look in my bed tonight
                        and find
my brothers and sisters gone

                        and the curdled glaze
of everafter on my father's skin
is cold as ice.

I love my love with an X
                        and here she comes, now, now,
stealing across the fields and creeping round

to feed

        my mouth
a sweet spot in the dark

she thinks is safe
                        until I drink her in.

OH NO, NOT MY BABY

But who is this other, waiting in the dark,
the one she listens for?
No ordinary man, but Brother Bones
calling to her in whispers from a place
she's known since girlhood: miles of perfect snow
to cancel out the fever of a body.
What treasured story makes her love the cold?
Some hallowed father, hunting in the blood?
Old wives-and-mothers, stitched along the marrow?

Everyone wants to tempt Providence, but she was lost
before we knew that lost was possible
and something in the woods, unkempt
and knowing, not
one body, but an undivided host
of looks and cries was waiting for its time
to drag her down, in some exquisite fall
to icebound realms
of hyacinth and vellum.

Sliding away in dreams she had rehearsed
for years, that tomboy sweetness in her face
of one struck dumb with awe, she shed her veils
in endless rounds of theme and variation,
but everything she touched returned to dust
and scattered to the wind as, at the end,
she scattered from my hands, no longer hurt
so beautifully, she seemed more song than woman.

MOON GOING DOWN

I have a dream.
                    She's in an attic room
with someone else,

hands in her skirt and that
dove sound caught in her throat

that I thought was ours.
She's with him now, she bends into his kiss

– and when she slows his hand, they swarm
like bees,

a honeyslick, an
aftergloss of meadow;

easy and damp,
though not without a trace

of venom, they are pure
as animals and

selfless,
like the rhythm in the heat

that, now and then, mistakes itself
for hunger;

and blessèd, strung like pearls on molten wire,
to bell and cry beneath a hunting moon,

they come together; live; unwarranted;
a braid in every touch, a flame for longing.

DAY OF THE DEAD

It's the corpse-groom
who holds my attention:

HansChristianAndersened
out of his wedding night
with the moth-eaten bride,

he's pledging his troth, by default,
to a marzipan doll

with eyes that no longer
remind him of someone else;

and, happy to be free
of hope and fear,

he listens for the wind
that snakes across

the asphalt, hymns
and ghost towns in its wake

and silence trailing after, like the sleep
he thought would end

in sugarcraft and satin.

DOWN BY THE RIVER

El muro cano
Va a imponerme su ley, no su accidente.
Jorge Guillén

She dies in a local flurry of dismay
as kittens do, held steady in a pail
of icy water,

never what I intended, more a case
of inattentiveness than grief or rage,

I held her in the current, fingers wound
with shift and slither.

It wasn't personal. It wasn't something planned.
I let her slip away, then stood, alone,

forgetting how the mind will travel far
to catch itself in blood and narrative:

a little thing; not mean, but
local, like a dustfall

or a blinding,
thought burning out in the eyes and the afterwards

that lasts too long,
like cinders in the rain.

It wasn't personal; I only saw
the logic in the moment of my bidding,

a slow tide, like the pull of earth and sky
that gripped her in my hands, and held her down,

inevitable, known but unforeseen,
imposing neither chance, nor accident.

A GAME OF MARBLES

The things I love
I bury in the woods
to keep them safe.
The pearl-effect,
the cherry-red and gold,
that touch of her
like tallow
on my skin.

Her sister
gives me silks
and Calla flowers,
I win a princess
and a devil's eye
and bury them alive
while she is
sleeping.

The earth turns cold,
my fingers brush the dead,
over the trees
a blue moon
sails through the sky.
I dig through leaf and mould,
I dig through bone,
slivers of glass
and ashes in the rain

and afterwards
the woods are like
a hymn
that, when I think of it,
I think of her:
the oxblood of her mouth,

her silver tongue,
milk on her fingers,
the hurry of pain
in her eyes.

CREATURELY

The only gift is knowing we belong
to nothing.

Midsummer's night
in the drunk tank, moon on the walls

and something like a fox scouting for mice
in the corner: shy

and auburn, it's the secret animal
I reckon from a childhood

resurrexit;
and why would there not

be weather, some
event like wind, or rain,

from thirty years ago?
The fox turns in the light with something slender

caught between its jaws and no one knows
for certain what it is: the one rule, here,

that no one leaves until the creaturely
in everything is sifted from his skin

to mark the cure, the rollright in the mind.

BIRD NEST BOUND

In the slow time, after the end, all you want
is home,

hopping a bus at a crossroads in the rain,
taking a stranger's car and lighting out

for somewhere you think you'll know
when the need arises.

Miles of scrub, a single, sun-parched
cottonwood, now and then,

or woods mile-deep in snow
and quiet, like the last thought in a dream

and, everywhere you go, the pleading voice,
the bloodless hand, the eyes lost in the current.

★

Day of the dead. The train leaves at 5 a.m.
Scatters of leaf and husk on an empty road
after a night of storms, that demi-sense
of winter coming, fencelines apple-sweet
and silk-white in the hollows.

Silk, I remember; silk and the pocketbook scent
of Philadelphus, innocent and long
familiar: wives being
mothers from a child's dream
all along,

the loves I left behind, inconstant girls
lost in the blue of evening, lost in their beds,
the scent of them, the pink and organdie
a world apart I never knew was mine
until I bowed my head, and spoke my vows.

★

I wake next day, at first light, bleared with the sense
of having been someone else,

not in the dream so much as in
the fit between sleep and waking,

the true self walking away, through a woodland clearing,
the air so still, it seems he's chanced upon

an old belonging, something he couldn't believe
till now.
       Safe sweet home, sweet home, through that shinin' star

And I wake, in the cage of my bones,
on the same cold ground.

FAITH

*But faith, like a jackal, feeds among the tombs,
and even from these dead doubts she gathers her
most vital hope.*

Herman Melville

FAITH

The tent show had been and gone
and now there was nothing but rust
and sunlight, like a poultice on the grass,
candy and broken glass
and a spare
tatter of hallelujah
blown through the dust

wherè somebody passing through
had stopped to write
a half-dozen half-formed letters
we couldn't decipher
out where the trailers had stood
at the edge of the night;

and the May Queen was lost for hours
before she was missed,
her mother asleep after back-shift,
her father a rumour,
a story the woman would tell
of a distant summer;
idealised, hazy at best,

he had left her one morning at dawn
for the Sanskrit of rain.
Go far enough, they say,
and some hideous god
will meet you, like a shadow on the road;
go further still, and scripture closes in:

a run of sodden fields, an empty street,
the last few houses white and incomplete
like houses in an early Flemish
painting, lamplit

windows rimmed with soot,
a bright canal and figures skating out
to distances where anything could vanish.

The woman never hears of them again,
the man long gone,
the daughter going after;
she sits up in the dark and prays for faith,
the strength she needs to say
they are together,

but sometimes, when she dreams, she comes upon
a scuffed trail in the woods, a beaten track
where something killed was dragged and trodden down
and hidden in the leaves. Its eyes are blind,
and what it clutches
in its broken hand,
is painfully familiar, shreds of black

and steel-grey, like that overcoat he wore
the day he left.
She wakes to mourning doves, a hint of blue,
thin sunlight on the walls and, at her door,
a figure she has never seen before,
not him, not her, but something of the two

combined – and then the shape she glimpsed is gone:
no memory of either, for a long
still moment, as the usual day begins:
the unhymned hours of work, the swoop of grief,
the moment's pause for utter disbelief,
fresh venom in whatever peace she wins,
the random acts of love, the venial sins.

HEARSAY

At the back of my mind, there is always
the freight-line that no longer runs
in a powder of snow

and footprints
from that story we would tell
of the girl from the next house but one

who should have been tucked up in bed
when she went astray,
a huddle of wool in the grass, or a silver bracelet

falling for days
through an inch and a half
of ice.

Nothing I know matters more
than what never happened:
the white at the back of my mind and the legends we made

of passing cars, or switchyards in the rain,
or someone we saw by the wire,
on an acre of ragweed,

acting suspicious, or lost, where the arc-lights decayed
and the souls of the dead went to dust
in a burrow of clinker.

HYENA

Like something out
of Brueghel, maned in white
and hungry
like the dark, the bat
ears pricked, the face
a grey

velour, more cat
than dog, less
caracal
than fanalouc
or civet –

here is the patron beast
of all
who love the night:
waking at dusk
to anatomy's
blunt hosanna,

the carrion daylight
broken
then picked to the bone
while the radio dance-band fades
to a slow alleluia,

and far at the back
of the mind, the perpetual
frenzy: eye-teeth
and muzzle
coated with blood
with matter,

as every mouth
digs in,
for fair, or foul,
a giggle in the bushes,
then a shudder.

NEOCLASSICAL

for Jonathan Barker

When they were flesh and blood, these deities
were local, like the fauna: oddly cruel,
yet human in their faults and, if not quite
dependable, then mischievous, at least,
in ways we understood, some imp or sphinx
probing the life it would mar
with delicate talons,
another form of love or self-defeat
unfolding in the dark
like fleece, or fire.

Now, there is nothing but white
and that lull in the stone
that makes us think of beauty going under,
a myth of naming buried in their eyes
and everything else immersed
in a drowse of heat:
frogs in the marguerites and the wakened
hedgehog at the far edge of the park,
hunting for snails
in a river of wind and yarrow;

and this is the grief
our stories prepared us for,
a ghost in the undergrowth,
hungry for nectar and blood,
and something we ought to have known,
without being told,
slinking towards us
out of the afternoon,
tender and wild
and blind to our fondest desires.

We have too much to gain from the gods, and this is why
they fail to love us,
turning away, like parents who cannot conceal
their disappointment, knowing, from the first,
that we are doomed, as they are, to a stark
momentum: something hidden in the grass
outwearing us, who never know our fates,
and drowning them, in abstract, like the dreams
they once replaced, in waves of moss and ivy.

AMNESIA

It never lasts;
but for a while,
at least,
I forget
what I wanted to see
from my kitchen door
and watch the new snow
falling in the yard,
precise
and random
like an early film,
whiting the corners
first,
then the spars
of the gate,
erasing the path
by degrees
and blanking out
the post-and-wire
along our boundary
till everything
is one
wide
incognito;
and all the world
is local: fuzzed
daguerreotypes
of motion
and those long
exposures
where a man
is almost there,
raising his hand
to wave,

or turning back,
precise
and random
like an early film
and pausing
in the snow,
as if to listen –

THE LISTENER

Luke 11:6

It's nightfall again on our hill.
Headlamps and spots of gold
in the middle distance;
sculleries; pig sheds; a bedroom above a yard
where someone is lulling an only child
to sleep.
I've been on this road since morning,
the land gone from green through grey
to a soft, damp bronze
around me till, a mile or so from home,
I come to the usual
gloaming: an almost white
against the almost black
of gorse and may.
Summer now: an older mode of sleep;
and this, the running dream that follows stone
and fence wire, digging in
for what remains of snow-melt and the last
good rain, the low road
peopled with bone-white figures: not
the living, in this aftermath of grass,
and not the dead we mourn, in empty kirks
or quiet kitchens, halfway through the day,
but something like the absence of ourselves
from our own lives,
some other luck
that would not lead
to now.
Along the coast, it's still
from field to field,

the living asleep or awake
in the sweat of their beds,
hard-wired with love
and salt-sweet from the darkness,
the long-dead blanking the roads
and everything
disloyal to the earth
it came from, streaks and nubs
of grief pooled in the dark
and stitched with strictest
pleasure at the core: that cunning
relish for the irremediable.
There's nothing so final as want
on a summer's night,
and few things so tender or sure
as a knock at the door
and nobody starting awake
in the knit and tear
of buried rooms, but
something long
contained, like that movie we saw
of mice that had bred
in their millions
scrambling away
through ruptured drains
and root-bins, nightlong squeals
for miles beneath the stains
of manganese and nickel in a wall
where ancient conversations turn to hair
and plaster: uncles
calling from the sway
of grammar
and a cousin twice-removed
reciting what she knows of saints and stars
for no one but herself,

resigned to live
forever, on the promises she kept
and paid for,
in a cradle
of thin air.

PIETER BRUEGHEL: WINTER LANDSCAPE WITH SKATERS AND BIRD TRAP, 1565

Learn from this picture how we journey in the world
Slithering as we go, the foolish and the wise

We have to imagine the duties they leave behind
for the thrill of the river,
the kitchens and middens, the sheepfolds and clouded byres,
the old folk in their sick beds
mumbling prayers.

The day is bright
and this is their escape
from hardship,
but each has his private hurt, her secret dread:
the man who starts thirsty and tired, his body soured
with last night's schnapps,
then skates out to the bridge at breakneck speed,
away from the loveless matron he's had to endure
for decades;
the woman in blue and grey, keeping pace with her child,
untroubled for now, but never released from the fear
that her husband will catch her wasting his precious time
and beat her as he's beaten her for years,
the moment he gets her home.

At midstream, the children play
with makeshift hockey sticks and, near the church,
a man finds the thoughtless grace
of the boy he once was
to glide free
in the very eye of heaven;
it could be simple – paradise foreseen –
but up on the rightmost bank, amid thorns and briars,

someone has built a bird trap from a plank
set on a perch, from which a length of rope
snakes to a half-closed door,
and all around it, birds dip from the air,
starlings and fieldfares, redwings, unaware
of any danger.

It seems a fable and perhaps it is:
we live in peril, die from happenstance,
a casual slip, a fault line in the ice;
but surely it's the other thought that matters,
the sense that, now and then, there's still a chance
a man might slide towards an old
belonging, momentarily involved
in nothing but the present, skating out
towards a white
horizon, fair
and gifted with the grace
to skate forever, slithering as he goes,
but hazarding a guess that someone else
is close beside him, other to his other.

COMMUNITY POOL

They come scattering out to the sky
like fireflies, lit with the green

of the deep end, my own
as random and shy as the others: shy

of themselves, being strange to themselves
and not altogether

the cumbersome mammals they were
when they shrugged off their clothes

and descended into the water, recovering
mangrove and marsh, and the sonar that runs in the spine

like a simmering touch, the extinct
and the still-to-come

radioed out in their hands
while the dark floods in

to drowse in the quick of them, homebound
and suddenly quiet.

WEATHER REPORT

A chill grey over our heads
at summer's end;
the road like a ditch

at Beley: aquaplane
and sidelights through the smirr
of afternoon;

yard brushes lost
in the mud
and carrion

hay on the fields,
where crows go
to pick at the drowned.

This is the weather, today,
and the weather to come;
the boys with their hands

to the glass, making perfect
phantoms of themselves
in their own steam,

or lodged in the doorframe,
they wave,
through the slantwise of rain,

already half-persuaded of a life
they never bargained for
and cannot alter.

INSOMNIA IN SOUTHERN ILLINOIS

If the mind is like a hall in which thought
is like a voice speaking, the voice is always that
of someone else.

Wallace Stevens

Out in the dark, over the snow,
a barred owl flits
through the cottonwoods, slow
and far in the distance, no matter how close

to the window it comes, its pit-black call
more echo than threat, where the mind is a hall
and thought is the voice
of another.

No one's awake: there's a gap on the stairs
where something is gone: say a grandfather clock,
or a previous householder, wandering back
to the life he had here;

and stealthily, as the night haunts round,
the porch light dwindles, without a sound
and, out in the darkness, over the snow,
the tracks of the mule deer come and go,

though nothing is there when I go to look,
only the churn of a passing truck
and that sense of the animals paused in the dark
till my eyes grow tired and the blind falls back

and the barred owl calls from the well of my mind,
more echo than thought, as it fades through the wind
and flickers away to the silence beyond
like the voice, in myself, of another.

THE SOUL AS THOUGHT EXPERIMENT

Some days, it's enough to stand your ground.
Wind on the road and that coal oil and mackerel sheen
on everything you see; the wet

leylandii turned in the rain, like the fur-lined gaps
in children's books;
                  the blood eyes in the wall
no longer what you feared, but sweet as love

and feral, like the soul you disallow
to call this home.
It's winter now, and late in the afternoon,

but though it's a long shot, you still believe someone will call
from far out in the hills, the moonlight falling
sidewise through a casement, as she speaks

of history and colour, celadon
and murrey, and those days of ironwood
or ginkgo, where you cannot help but think

of kinship, at the point where snow begins
on some black road you thought was yours alone,
made bright and universal, while you listen.

LATE SHOW

I only watch reruns now,
or films about geese,

and yet I'm waiting for the miracle
I used to find in early black and white

where everyone looks like us and ends up
happy, in a place they're learning

never to take
for granted.

In Northern Canada,
it's summer now

and birds that look like friends I had in school
are dancing in a field of moss and thaw

and, as I watch, the darkness gathers round me
slowly, warmth and quiet in its gift

for as long as the birds
take flight, or Lucille Ball

lights up the screen
like someone who's been there forever.

FROM THE CHINESE

Turn of the year
and a white Christmas turning to slush
on my neighbours' fields,

crows on the high road,
the yard streaked with coal dust
and gritting,

geraniums turning to mush
in the tubs and baskets.

I walk to the end of the road
to ease my sciatica:
ditch water, gorse bones; how did I get so cold

so quickly?

Thaw in the hedge
and the old gods return to the land
as buzzard and pink-footed goose and that

daylong, perpetual scrape
of winter forage;

but this is the time of year
when nothing to see
gives way to the hare in flight, the enormous

beauty of it stark against the mud
and thawglass on the track, before
it darts away, across the open fields

and leaves me dumbstruck, ready to be persuaded.

NOTES & ACKNOWLEDGEMENTS

Black Cat Bone: A powerful hoodoo talisman, conferring success, invisibility and sexual power on its owner. It is highly prized because of the elaborate and dangerous nature of the rite by which it is obtained; cf. Zora Neale Hurston's *Mules and Men* for a vivid account of the ritual.

The sequence uses quotes from works by the Reverend Gary Davis and Charlie Patton, among others.

'Princess' and 'Devil's Eye' are types of marble.

Pieter Brueghel: Winter Landscape with Skaters and Bird Trap, 1565: The epigraph here is translated from an inscription added to Pieter Brueghel the Elder's *Skaters Before the Gate of St George* some hundred years or so after the work was made. The original runs:

> Aij leert hier aen dit beeldt, hoe wij ter wereldt rijen
> En slibberen onsen wegh, d'een mal en d'anders wijs

Insomnia in Southern Illinois: This poem quotes freely from Edward Thomas' 'Out in the dark', the first poem I ever got by heart.

Acknowledgements are due to *Agenda, London Review of Books, Paris Review* and *The Times Literary Supplement*.

'The Fair Chase' was commissioned by *Scotland on Sunday* for the anthology, *Headshook*. 'Loved and Lost' was commissioned by BBC Radio 3.